GRANDMAS
& GRANDPAS

A gift book written by children for grandparents everywhere

Edited by Richard & Helen Exley

▤EXLEY

Grandpas are special because they cym up stairs and cis you in bed.

Rachel Healy   Age 5

Other titles in the series:
TO MOM (USA), TO MUM (UK, Australia)
TO DAD,
HAPPY BIRTHDAY! (you poor old wreck),
CATS (and other crazy cuddlies)

Second Edition published 1990

First edition published in Great Britain
in 1975, revised and updated 1990 by

**Exley Publications Ltd,
16 Chalk Hill, Watford, Herts WD1 4BN,
United Kingdom.**

Copyright © Richard and Helen Exley, 1975
Copyright © Richard and Helen Exley, 1990

ISBN 1-85015-244-6

A copy of the CIP data is available from the
British Library on request.

First edition 1975
Second & third printings 1977
Fourth & fifth printings 1978
Sixth to eighth printings 1980
Ninth & tenth printings 1981
Eleventh printing 1982
Twelfth printing 1983
Thirteenth printing 1984
Fourteenth printing 1985
Fifteenth printing 1986
Sixteenth & seventeenth printings 1988
Eighteenth printing 1989
Nineteenth printing 1990

Second edition 1990
Second & third printings 1991
Fourth printing 1992

Designed by Richard Exley.
Front cover drawing by Joanne Bunn, age 8.
Back cover drawing by Gemma Busby, age 6.

Printed and bound in Hungary.

Grandparents ... fill in the gap that mothers and fathers leave out.

This is the book that launched our publishing company. We had little idea when this book first appeared in the 1970s that it would prove so abidingly popular, reprinting year afer year as successive generations of families recognised the funny, candid, loving and sometimes cryptic portrayal of grandparents by their grandchildren.

Now we have edited the book for the 1990s. The writing shows that, of course, much remains the same. The things the children say confirm our belief that there is a very special bond between grandchildren and grandparents; grandparents "fill in the gap that mothers and fathers leave out", as one of the children put it.

All the entries and illustrations in the book are by children. Nothing has been changed – not even the sometimes amazing grammar and spelling. A few were badly written, or went on about grousy grandmas. But the overwhelming majority of entries tell a kind of love story; each one presents a personal little cameo, each one tells of a grandparent who is precious to a child. Sometimes the child doesn't seem to be aware of much more than the chocolates and the presents. Many of the entries from the younger children make grandma sound like a walking ice-cream factory. But very

soon, especially among the girls, something else emerges. They begin to appreciate the time a grandparent has to give. Many letters talked of gran or grandpa as a "best friend".

We've had great fun editing this new edition, and we hope it brings families everywhere great joy. The book is a kind of "Thank you" for all the bandaged knees, apple pies and bedtime stories – and the lessons in life so freely given. One summed up the feeling very simply: "We try to pay her back for her kindness to us. But it would take for ever."

Enjoy the book. The children say it all, with such perception.

Richard & Helen Exley

Grandmothers and Grandfathers give a home a friendly touch.

Marco Orlandini   Age 9

My christening gown was made from her wedding dress. History for me is memories for them, yet they are not aged or dusty: Grandma and Grandpa are real. A whole part of my childhood would be missing if I had not known them. With them I am at once a little girl and an object of pride and hope for the future.

E J Slessenger

Every time children go there most of them say "come in deary hallo pet" and all lovely words like that. Sarah Keen   Age 8

Joanna Simmonds

Catherine Jones   Age 10

7

Definitions

A grandfather is the one who helps you with your homework, even when he doesn't know how to do it. Gary

Your grandad is the one that tries to make you tough. But when you try to be tought, you get beat up.

Bradley Simpson Age 12

A Grandmother is a lady who either sleeps or knits.

Sara Spurrier Age 12

A Grandmother corrects your grammar and wipes immaginary dirt from your cheeks. K Phillips Age 11½

Grandmothers are people who still do the spring cleaning.

Maureen Dracey

She's the person who tells me all the things about my parents, they would rather not have me know.

Sarah Scott Age 15

My Grandpa is tough outside, but soft hearted inside.

Justin Birch Age 10

Grandparents are cheerful, sentimental old things.

Donna Pearce Age 12

Andrew Age 9

The dictionary says, quite simply, a grandmother is "a father's or mother's mother" but had there been room, I'm sure they would have added ...
Grandmothers are

Generous giving people
Regular churchgoers
Afternoon snoozers
Never (well, hardly ever) irritated by you
Drinkers of whisky and water
Members of a ladies' church group
Owners of old jalopies
Crossword fanatics
Hospitable hostesses
Eaters of brocolli, spinach, cabbage and beans
Relaters of gossip
Scrabble players

and without Grandmothers, the world would be a different place.

H Bulley

Mark Marvis Age 9

A Grandmother is kind and doesn't like all the new coins and other small change – she gives us them quite happily.

Bobby Marston

A Grandmother doesn't criticize.

Anne Joplin Age 11½

Gram's always have something up their sleeve like gum drops.

Gemma Cummings Age 10

Grandmothers wander around and look very suspicious. Grandmothers' bones are old.

Caroline Curtis Age 11

Emma Witham Age 7

A GRANDMOTHER

Simon Steer   Age 11

My Grandmother is a knitting machine. Carolynn Shaw　Age 7

Grandma's and Grandad's hardly ever tell you off so you have to look at your feet, with your head hung down and hands clenched together. They let you off as light as a feather.

Jennifer Norman　Age 12

My Grandparnts are very nice to me.
When we leave they cry. Vanessa Coppeck　Age 9½

A Grandmother is a little old lady, who comments on the weather and how tall you are getting, tells everyone the latest gossip and all about her son who came to see her. She lets you do what you shouldn't and if mom complains she says "Remember when you were little and I caught you dipping your finger in the sugar bowl? You're not too old to get your ears boxed".

Jackie Thompson

There is one thing that bothers me it is my gran hadly ever gose out because she is to old to go on the back of the moter bike.

Lenny　Age 9

Candy　Age 6

12

Appearance

My Grandmother is crumpled.

Richard Humphrey

Some grandmothers are very small and some grandmothers are bery big. You can get all different sized grandmothers, you know.

Andrew Deboata   Age 8

The thing that makes grandmas so jolly looking is the fact that as they get older they grow out instead of up.

Jacqueline Hope

A grand-father is a verey old person and they can not walk verey fast but there skin is not verey thik and you can see there bones.

Kevin Bewick   Age 7

My Grandma is a little fat but Nowa-days most Grandmas are.

Alan Richards   Age 9

Mine looks funny. She has got a long face and her chin wobbels when she walks.

Michael Barbridge   Age 7

My grandparents aren't all crooked and bent. But I doubt if they're old enough yet. I don't think they will ever seem very old to me.

Philip Paddon   Age 12

A grandmother can be tall or small but mine is midium and cuddly fat.

Catherine Cardwell   Age 9

Mostly sympathetic

A Grandmother is an elderly person who watches people walk past and hopes that someone will come and visit them.

Simon Martindale   Age 10

Grandmothers are the old in the world of the young, and are continually having the "good old days" wiped out of the conversation. They long to help and yearn to be loved.

Rita Bourke

My Great Grandad has a habit of buying me chocolates and then eating them.

Jay Coquillon   Age 11

Grandmothers always come up with advice, which is given whether you need it or not.

Rita Bourke

Claire Parry   Age 11

Julia

Grandmothers used to be formal, strict, old fashioned and covered in slippery black dresses tinkling with jet trinkets and smell of mothballs. My father's mother is a grandmother but she is comfortable and warm and soft, scented with cologne and baking.

E J Slessenger

As you have proberly noticed my granny thinks time stands still and wears the same clothes as when she was small (except a few sizes bigger).

Paul Milsom   Age 10

Grandmothers wear quite long coats to cover up their knobbly knees.

Carol Stacey   Age 7

A Grandmother tells you to put on a coat or you will catch a cold. A Grandmother fusses over you. A Grandmother wears old fashioned clothes.

Angela Mutch   Age 11

Allison

16

Sandra Dale   Age 9

17

Habits

Grandmothers are sort of a pest. They want everything so spick and span and neat.
Caroline Webb   Age 10

Grandmothers some times lock the door when they come out and when they get to the garden gate they go back to make sure they have.
Eunice Hopkins   Age 10

Grandmothers are fat and put wigs on before they go to the door.
Richard Dunmow   Age 8

My Grandma has a good habbit of eating cake every evening. I like this because I have some too.
Nicholas Dunne   Age 11

My Gram has a habbit of naming things she calles her freezer Fredda and her two radios big willy and little willy.
Allison Anthony   Age 10

When my mother gets thirsty she has a cup of tea but when my granma gets thirsty she has a gin and tonic.
Jackie Holleley   Age 10

My Grandma has some very extraordinary habbitts.
David Heys   Age 10

Perhaps the best definition of the grandmother, is somebody who spent her time telling your mother what not to do, when she was young. And now spends her time, criticism your mother for giving you the same advice.
Calvin Giles   Age 12

Mine knits all the time, though we have socks for more than 10 years.
Anette Bromner   Age 14

Jacqueline Hollely   Age

She's got oblong eyes because she watches television all day.

Sandra Rendell   Age 10

Now she needs me

My grandmother is a box of
childrens building blocks
Each a different size and shade
Each one different from the other.

When I was young and cut my knee
She would become an enfolding, purple curve of sympathy.

If I was caught doing, any wrong thing
She would be a rectangle, dark blue glowing.

If in dire need of help am I
She is a pulsating orange pillar,
That touches the sky.

When something special I have
Into a bouncing restless globe, she will go
Of a beautiful sunflower yellow.

To the dismal depths of depression I have been
So she has become a pyramid of gentle green.

When she is ill
And I make her jovial
A blazing turquoise star,
tells me I'm her cheering up pill.

Funny, and strange, how time should change.
Amazing how time should beg
I needed her once now she needs me.

Quentin Radford   Age 11

The nice thing about her, is that she says that I've got two homes, my home and their home.

Julia Gambold   *Age 9*

Brigid Cooper   *Age 7*

Some peoples grandmas are tough old ladies, if you say they are too old to do something, they will say "Don't be silly, I could walk a mile in a minite".

Belinda Spark   Age 11

Some grandmas are the kind that look frail on the outside, but on the inside they are the dangerous kind, that bash policemen and robbers on the head with umbrellas and handbags if they get angry.

Belinda Spark   Age 11

My Granny is very game for her age. I distinctly remember, one day, when she took me on an outing to a park, and she said to me, shall we run round the Fish Pond, shouting at the top of our voices? and when I asked her why, she said she felt like doing something naughty.

Jane Townson   Age 10

Stuart Ross   Age 9

24

Neil Grant   Age 10

Grandpas

Grandad is mad about Football he was a player once but now he is to old so when he trys to kick a ball sometimes he falls over.

Kaal Page   Age 9

Grandads are very lazy and sit back smoking and watch old westerns. Some grandads stay asleep all day until they feel hungry then they wake up. After supper they go back to sleep. My Grandad calls me ham bonse.

Mark Ward   Age 9

My Grandfather is a funny sort of character because every time I go down to his house to borrow somthing for my Mother he says "No" and then lets me borrow it.

Colin McRae   Age 11

My Grandad pretends he has a jelly bean tree.

William Sholl   Age 8

Grandpas always have a bag of tasty goodies in their pockets well as lots of junk and odds and ends, such as a penknife, string, a compass, an animal bone and a toy soldier.

Fiona Gibbings

Grandfathers like cabbage and caulieflower and other awful things.

Beth   Age 10

My grandad teases me a lot but realy he is not a teaser but just a kind old man.

Mark Moulding   Age 8

My Grandpa used to rough and tumble with my brother But now both of them are past it.

Richard Thompson   Age 12

Inflation
Inflation they say
not like the
good old days.

Catherine Ashley   Age 9

Andrew Barnett   Age 10

27

My grandmommy loves my granddad and my granddad loves my grandmommy. Sometimes they get mad at each other and they fight. I feel bad. When they get lovey dovey again and kiss I feel good.

Kimberley   Age 5

The only time my grandma is sad is when she washes Grandads socks.

Natalie Hall   Age 9

A grandad is a earbox for a grandmother to say things to.

Nicola Hankinson   Age 11

Elise Moss   Age 8

Sarah Barnes   Age 9

Grumblers and grumps

My Grandma is always saying don't touch, put that book away don't read in bed or something like that. She sayse put that car away. pick that up don't drew in that reading book. and at bedtime she even does it more. Go to sleep or you will be late for school in the morning, be quite, don't play with that, don't rip the blankets and then its brechfast time dreedfull don't lick your dish, brush your teeth wash your hands. I'm glad when I get to school and I don't hurry home. when I get home she starts again. did you get some stares yes Grandma. How many? Five. not good enough. and at bed time she starsts again.

Dawn   Age 7

Perhaps her most peculiar obsession was the sending back of letters. Whenever I wrote to her I would receive my letter back with red lines underneath each word I had spelt wrong. So I had to rewrite the letter correctly and if I spelt anything wrong again back the letter would come, with the same red lines again. Obviously one would write to her as little as possible.

Amanda Bond

Grandpa is usauly the grumpest of the pair. He is kind but not as kind as your nana.

Elspeth Bridges

My Fathers Mother is rather grumpy she likes to watch the news and moans to us when she hears about bombs as if we had planted them.

Allison Anthony   Age 10

Grandmoms are awkward and they never want to do what other pepull are doing.

David Hoggarth   Age 9

30

Some people may think grandma's are special. I don't think grandma's are special they are just relatives.

Steven Alan Jones   Age 8

Some days when we've been there two long they should be called a new names Grumppa and Groanie.

Alberto Fernandez   Age 8

Diane Barnett   Age 7

Grannies used to be old with grey hair. But nowadays grannies can be quite young.

Amanda Weisberg   Age 7

About age

Grandmas say that the title makes them feel old – like a Grand piano, I suppose. As an alternative, how about Supermom?

Isobel Blaber   Age 14

My Grampa looks very old to me and my brother.

Trevor Cox

My Grandparent's are both conciderate. They are both about the same age but that doesn't seem to bother them.

Elizabeth Rose

A Grandma is very nice and is some-time's old.

Lynne J Gregory   Age 9½

My grandmother is getting older than she thinks.

Clive Owen   Age 10

Grandpa is over 40 and under 90.

Alexander Hambly   Age 10

Grammas always act young and seem young but are old.

Lucy Deamer

They aren't young, But my dad's catching up.

N Arthur   Age 13

When they tell my parents Not to be childish I feel very, very young.

Peter Wilson   Age 12

When she is sitting by herself she looks old and lonely. But when she has company she looks young again.

Mary O'Gorman   Age 11

I Thought Dad was rather old – untill I met grandpa.

Ian Laing   Age 13

I wonder does she feel young inside.

Catherine Lawlor   Age 11

my grandpa and grandma love each other because they hold hands and he keeps telling her silver threads among the gold.

Sarah Anderson, Age 8

this is my grandad in the garden getting some flowers for my granma.

34

Robert Edwards Age 7

A fascination with teeth

My Grandma has special toothpaste and pretending teeth.

Clive Smith   Age 7

Once she lost her teeth later when I was running the bath they floated to the top. I think she is very typical.   *S Enright*

They often have a few false teeth Which in the morning are often found out Which lie besides the bed which are quite frightening They look like elephants fangs.   *Helen Turner*

If theres one thing that annoys me about her is, she clicks her false teeth and she does it when theres any music going keeping in time with the tune.   *Alison Brice*

A Grandad is some one who undermines a parents authority. He has a habit of clicking his false teeth.

Philip Hooper   Age 11

My Grand Mother is very unusual.
She has a very funny face.
Shes got silver hair and only four teeth left.
I fink she should have two teeth out that
will leave two.   *David Fitzgibbon   Age 7*

My Grandma has false teeth I do not like the look of her when she's got them out.   *Richard Morrey   Age 8*

I thing My Grand-dads great, he stayed with us all Christmas. He has no teeth and he hasn't got faulse teeth. When my Grand-dad laughs I can see the top of his gums and it makes me laugh to.   *Janette Wright*

My grandma hates false teeth. She is scared her dinner will get stuck underneath.

Steven Whiskin   *Age 8*

"Will you look at that" shouted Grandpa and took out his false teeth and shook them at the driver who had just passed us. (Grandpa does not like being passed he hardly ever is though because he drives at such a speed). When we came up behind him, Grandpa waved his false teeth and shouted "You crazy old fool".

D Farnworth

Andrew Clissold   *Age 12*

Food and cooking

She cooks delishush diners.

Michael Barbridge   Age 7

Nans are people who give you cream and waffles and watery orange drink and expects you to eat it all.

Susan Garmston

My grandmother makes lots of cakes, but the nicest thing about that is she lets me put the decorations on the top.

Tanya Burch   Age 9½

Grandmothers fruit cakes are more fruit than cake mixture.

Jane Hitchcock

She makes real gateau and cake which never fall flat like my mothers.

Sarah Richardson   Age 10½

My Grandmother is a good cook. Choklitikake is my best feest when I go to stay.

Mark Harris   Age 9

A faint aroma of gingerbread and all good things mixed together, seems to linger all around a grandmother.

Elspeth Gordon   Age 12

Rachel Williams

40

Reginald

The best thing that I like about my Grandmother is, when she gets up in the morning and the heater's on she'll come and get dressed there. She'll stand by the heater and warm her behind and then my grandpa will come along and he stands there looking at me and then he looks at Grandma and he then gives a funny laugh, then creeps up to her and he rubs her fat tummy
"Reginald" she shouts.
Her face then glows and wrinkles up and her eyes are full of laughter, her cheeks are a pair of roses and her glasses fall on to her nose.
"Reginald", she shouts, "if you don't stop that I'll have a burn't behind.

Beverly Ward

Militant Grannies

They appear on the strikers camp, with rolling pins
All armed to the teeth,
All ready to do battle with gnashing teeth,
One granny lets go with her Fiery left hook,
Which lands a union leader in the pond,
Where he floats on his back, like a dead duck,
They swing out left and right
With all their might,
And strike down every enemy in their sight,
And as the strikers Flee the scene.
Then the grannies take up the chase,
They swing their handbags like a mace
They smash them down, one by one,
And as each one Falls,
All the grannies let out their victory calls.

Adrian John Bradley   *Age 12 years 9 mths*

Sarah Woolston   Age 9

How can she make them understand?

She sits there living,
In her memories,
The young men, the laughter
The river boats,
Summer picnics and romance,
Romance unlike any other,
Special, strong and
Everlasting.

Nothing is left now,
Only memories,
Though life goes on, but
She cannot understand
Remembering her long quiet childhood,
Which no longer remains,
Life was simple,
And days were long and happy
Children now are so restless
And unloving, taking everything
For granted, awaiting their maturity
Wasting their long, lazy days
Of innocence
Oh, how can she make them understand?

Susan Legg   Age 15

Sarah Fraser   Age 7

Grandpas

A Grandad is a person you never forget, never.
I'm proud that he's my grandad.
And I'll never forget his hand in mine as we walk down the street together.

Suzanne Cairns   Age 13

I think my grandpa is fantastic, most grandpas are. If you are saving up for something they are like walking piggy banks and give you money.

Jeremy Shilling

I love the magic Grandad does, especially the peppermints he makes appear from my ear!

Rebecca Smith   Age 11

Grandpa grows great rasberries and always pretends not to notice us eating them.

Tracey Knight   Age 8

He cares for everything,
Everything,
But himself.

Joanna Read   Age 12

My Grandfather always falls to sleep after the football results are over, and he wakes up when he hears his buzz word "food".

Stephen Mouncher   Age 11

My grandfather is not really like any old man, for he is 86 years old and has a special driving license and swims in ice cold lakes in which I would never dare to put my foot. A person must not think of him as a first class madman, or at least a person can think as a person wants but I still think and will think he is the nicest and most considerate person I have had to bump into.

P Ham   Age 13

My grandad is very kind he alway lifts me up when I fall over.

Caroline Fish

A grandfather is somebody who outbalds Kojak.

Nicholas

Samantha Weinstein   Age 9

Belinda Sacks   Age 9

My Grandma and Grandpa

ndmas and Grandpas are very kind to you.

Sometimes they keep you talking when you're
a rush to leave. But they can't help it I suppose,
have two grandads and one grandma. My other grandma
in heaven but she was always helping other people
I know she is a very special angel.

Sharon Watson   Age 9

Your Granny loves you. No matter what you do.

Paul Myers Age 10

I have thought it out that the youngest a legal grandmother can be is thirty three and three quarters. This is not often the case. Normally they are in their late fifties or early sixties. To a young child, this seems ancient, but as they grow up, and watch their parents pushing the forties, they see how young they really are!

I always associate grandmothers with knitting and darning – very useful when you go through your socks at the rate I do! They are often widows and therefore have to be visited fairly often. If they drive, they are highly lethal – either driving too slowly or in the middle of the road (or both!) If and when they send you postcards from their seaside resort (where they go and visit great aunty Flo) their writing is always thin, wobbly, spidery and totally illegible. They feel the cold far too easily, require an electric blanket, thermal underwear, wooly long johns and the heat on in the middle of summer! Their cutlery is normally silver (whether they can afford it or not) and the table cloths and napkins are always stiffly starched.

They love potted plants, radio, television and old china ware. They have an annoying habit of never having their "spectacles" handy when they need them.

One big problem they all have in common is being very deaf. This means that everyone has to speak slowly and loudly for them to hear. When given a hearing aid for a Christmas present they complain when you speak too loud!

At meal times even though they eat very little, they feel obliged to leave something (an old fashioned habit I believe) which is very annoying indeed.

On the whole despite their annoying ways, I like grandmothers very much, knowing that someday I'll probably end up like them!

L Horne   *Age 13*

A grandpa is the person who helps you eat your food when you can't eat it all, so it looks like you at it all.   Farrah   *Age 10*

My Grandmother is very patient. She would have to be with me around!   Helena Leeson   *Age 10*

Linda McLaughlin   *Age 9*

49

A grandma is old on the outside and young on the inside.

John Wright   Age 7½

A Granny is jolly and when she laughs a warmness spreads over you.

J Hawksley   Age 11

The age of my Grandma is young. She can do all the things around the house. She takes me to the park. My Grandma likes playing football and rollercoaster and loves running.

Mandy Tiwana   Age 11 years 3 months

Becky   Age 6

50

Donna Longville

Bribery

It's very noisy in our house and when Grandma comes over she says, If you can be quiet I'll give you some spending money. And we are quiet then for a little while.

Joe Cassidy   Age 12

Grandmas are very necessary for letting you do things you are not allowed to do generally, like watching "The Late Night Horror Movie" or eating too many waffles than are good for you, or not making you eat carrots.

Kate Clancy   Age 14

My granny lets me lick the cake mixture when she is finished. She lets me leave my food, and she spoils me so much that when I grow up I won't want anything.

Sandra Webb   Age 10

Most grandmothers will spoil you if they can, but parents will butt in just as you're about to eat your third helping of cake, it's awfully annoying.

Helen Schwendener   Age 11

The 'grandmother' is usually a great source of the children's income as she nearly always gives them quite a lot of money after a happy but exhausting visit. The money is usually for all her grand-children ("little angels"). They usually stick their hands out suggestively or start whining that they can't afford a teddy bear or a skiing trip.

Charles Robert Fenwick Linfoot   Age 13

Every time I went over to her house I got some more money. As I liked my grandmother I went over to her house about five times a week.

Andrew Austin   Age 10

Dad says you're spoiling us but do they listen oh no. Presents here presents there presents everywhere. I like Grandmothers spoiling me. Darlings they always say, while Dad, thinks what rubbish.

Catherine Ashley   Age 9

One of a grandmother's most prized privileges is to spoil her grandchildren. She arrives armed with pockets full of goodies, and special pocket-money to buy the child the things denied it by its parents for numerous good reasons – no cheesecakes because they have too much sugar for example. Granny stuffs the child full of ice cream and cakes, and then leaves before it is sick.

Tessa Ing

When my mother tells me to do something I do not want to do I tell my Grandmother and she talks my old lady out of it.

Sonia Allan   Age 10

My Granma lets us stay up and watch horror films. My Granma is really really really nice.

Mark Robinson   Age 9

Colin Fleetham   Age 11

Who can measure Grandmothers?

She seemed in a mask or costume
As much as a hat or glove.
For in her talk was youth and life
As pure as a beautiful dove.

Her mask was of wrinkled skin
Attached onto her face.
It was not really her because it did not fit
It belonged to another time and place.
But the more she talked and as I watched her
She shed the mask from her face.

A light as new as spring shone in her eyes
And in her movements a youthful grace.

Age is but a word of time
A thing which we created.
A thing which is measured like the bleeps on a radio.
But who can measure grandmothers
And put them into hours and minutes
Of knowledge kindness love and care?

The nearest measurement there is for me
Is that They are like the jewels in a watch
The watch is the world
And the wheels are the tools of the spring
The spring is life
The more jewels the better the watch.
My Grandmother is no diagem or paste
But a clear and sparkling diamond.

54

Jacqueline Solomons

A Grandmother

This small pale woman, a mother grown old,
By her hair and her wrinkles her age can be told,
Her past is a dream, an impossible hope,
For her children are married now and able to cope.
Her role as a mother has vanished and gone,
As the moon loses its role when up come the sun.

But the birth of a Grandchild means new life has begun.
The birth of a Grandmother, Parents and son.
Now there is a role, a part to be played
For this small pale woman, a grandmother is made.
New qualities of joy have begun to show
Is this the same woman whom I used to know?

She now is a grandmother, a person who shares
A person who loves and a person who cares,
Her face has an expression of understanding and love,
Of normal standards she towers above.
Her time to all is so generously given,
A person who I'm sure is destined for heaven.

Sally Lloyd Jones   Age 14

Cindy   Age 8

A Refuge

When you go to her with your pride bruised and hurt; she never takes sides, but helps you to think fairly and to see the other person's point of view. She knows the problems that all the members of her family go through, and is able, from her own experience to give advice.

She is usually a sympathetic listener – to what must seem to her, your personal inconsequential (compared with some of the ones that she has to face during her life-time) problems. She never tries to advise her children on grand-children, unless she is asked to do so, and lives her own life, far enough away, so as not to be a nuisance, but close enough (to her children) to be a help in a crisis. In short a grandmother is a refuge.

Amanda Evans

Grandparents live in their own funny world where time seems To go backwards.

Kevin J Brown Age 12

Yesterday

She's called "Nana" and she tells tales that she told to mother when she was a child. Many stories of exciting adventures that happened a long time ago. They did not have the luxuries that we have, but waltzing in their large living room when the furniture was pushed aside, singing round the piano, telling stories by the blazing fire whilst they ate hot muffins. Skating on the frozen lake in winter, riding in a steam train, all these more than make up for television and trips abroad. I hope my Nana will stay with me for a long time, and when I have the farm I long for, she will be able to live with me and feed the chickens. We will have a blazing log fire and she will tell us stories of the past.

Dawn Williams Age 10

Grandpas

Anthony Day   Age 10

When I go to my grandad's he says Kate Kate Kate and I say yes yes yes chatterbox and he says you silly billy and he tells me to do his buttons up and I say alright chatterbox.

Kate Sheppard   Age 7

If you want something always give your grandad a hug.

Claire Elaine Picken   Age 9

A grandfather is the only one who can call me "gimpy" without hurting my feelings.

Miles   Age 10

Andrew Smith   Age 6

Love

I would not want my grandma to go up to heaven.

Michael Orloff

My Grandmother is not plump but nice and comfortable, when she sits you on her knee you can nestle down and feel safe and secure.

Angela Dobson   Age 10

We call her Nanny. She is not very old
I don't mind how old she is.
I would not want another nanny because ours is the nicest one.
I wouldn't swop her for any sum of money.

Jane Clarke   Age 10

My grandma is in heaven but she was always helping other people so I know she is a very special angel.

Sharon Watson   Age 9

Grandmothers are very useful for showing you how to do lots of different stitches.

Caroline Webb

If I have a secret I will always tell Grandmother not anyone else.

Joanna Simmonds   Age 8

Dear old lady rich with our love forever, heart of our home, That's Grandmother.

Ursula O Leary   Age 11

You can tell them secrets of all the bad things you have done and they won't tell our mothers. Then they tell you about all the wicked things they did when they were little.

If we get bored with our mother and father telling us what to do, there's always someone waiting for us with her arms out.

Helen Tidy   Age 9

A Grandmother is a mother who has a second chance.

Caroline Flitcroft   *Age 11*

A grandmother is someone you love helping.

Jane Farrell   *Age 11*

Kim Curd   *Age 11*

Katy T   Age 8

All the time in the world

She has a past of her own and a future which belongs to everyone. She leads an empty life of her own which is filled by the lives of others. Most of all she is a person who will always have time to see you when the rest of the world is busy.

Gill Webb

Grandmas are always slow but they do not mind for they have all the time in the world.

Malcolm Andrew   Age 10

Grandmas and Grandpas have nothing to do
But talk to you.

Catherine Mellors

I love you because you are always happy for me to show you things other people don't bother to look at.

Katy Turner   Age 8